How To Use This Book

There are lots of extras in this book aimed at helping you win your next debate!

BRAIN JAM

Brain Jams offer activities to get you thinking creatively and give you a chance to hone your skills.

PROJECT JUMP START

Project Jump Starts provide that sometimes necessary extra push to get you going on your own debate.

TIP FILE

Tip Files offer up all sorts of helpful suggestions and hints on getting the project done.

RESOURCES   RESOURCES

One of these icons will lead you to more information.

ORDINARY   EXTRAORDINARY

Throughout the book, you will see the ordinary and the extraordinary side by side. With revisions and some thought, these comparisons show you what you can accomplish.

Many thanks for the comments, thoughts, advice, and guidance of the people who really have been there and done that: Nichole Bigley, Ben Garcia, Robert Jamie McKown, Sara Brueck Nichols, Dr. Mabry O'Donnell, Joe Patrice, Christine Pham, Chris Richter, Christi Siver, and Miranda Weigler.

Photographs © 2006 Corbis Images: 94 (Tim Graham), 19 (Mark Savage).

Cover design: Marie O'Neill
Series design: Simon Says Design and Marie O'Neill
Art production: The Design Lab
Cover and interior illustrations by Kevin Pope

Library of Congress Cataloging-in-Publication Data

Orr, Tamra B.
  Extraordinary debates / by Tamra B. Orr.
     p. cm. — (F.W. prep)
  Includes bibliographical references and index.
  ISBN 0-531-16763-1 (lib. bdg.)   0-531-13905-0 (pbk.)
  1. Debates and debating. I. Title. II. Series.
  PN4181.O66 2005
  808.5'3—dc22   2005020839

EXTRAORDINARY
Debates

by Tamra B. Orr

Franklin Watts®

A Division of Scholastic Inc.
New York • Toronto • London • Auckland • Sydney
Mexico City • New Delhi • Hong Kong
Danbury, Connecticut

EXTRAORDINARY DEBATES

THE PROJECT GUIDES REVEALED

ASSIGNMENT:

When your parents give you a curfew, it truly is because they care about you. They want you to be safe. In the same vein, when your teachers assign you a part in some form of debate, it is because they care about your future. They want you to learn the vital life skills that debate can teach you. You will call on those life skills to get accepted into college and do well when you are there. Those same skills will play a part in virtually any job you will ever have. As James Dittus and Miriam Davies write in their paper for the Speech Communication Association, "All persons, in all walks of life, must speak and defend ideas in public."

Debates are a part of the plan your state has for your education. Each state in the country has its own educational curriculum plan for you and other students in your state. These plans are called educational standards. From **Massachusetts** to **California,** from **North Dakota** to **Alabama,** the standards call for students to tackle a variety of debate projects. In Massachusetts, for instance, students are expected to be able to give both formal and informal talks employing the methods most

DEBATE

suitable for their audience. California wants students to be able to present clear thesis statements and back them up with appropriate types of proof.

So see, you're not alone. Thousands of other students are tackling Lincoln-Douglas debates, parliamentary debates, and many other types of debates. This means that like you, they are hitting the books, searching library shelves, and surfing the Internet. They are outlining, writing down their arguments, and practicing their speeches. So how do you make your debating skills stand out from all the rest? In a word, how do you make it EXTRAORDINARY?

Sprinkled throughout the book are one- and two-line tips from a variety of debate experts. These people have been there and done that, so listen up. The tips are golden!

Part of making any project EXTRAORDINARY —whether it's a research project, debate, or poem— is knowing what is expected of you and surpassing those expectations. Regard those expectations as opportunities for you to develop and express your own creative ideas while improving your skills as a writer and public speaker. Debating ideas is also useful preparation for your future. Expressing your ideas clearly in words or on paper will make you shine in any job.

Check Out Your State's Standards!

One way to stay ahead of the game is to take a look at your state's standards for this year and the years ahead. If you're ready to look into your future, try visiting the Developing Educational Standards site at: **http://www.edstandards.org/Standards.html** There you can find links to the educational departments of every state and even focus on language arts in particular.

For more of a national overview of language arts standards, let's take a look at a few of the twelve national educational standards created by the National Council of Teachers of English (NCTE). (For a complete list, visit NCTE's Web site, **http://www.ncte.org**.)

By researching and preparing extraordinary debates, you demonstrate several key skills mentioned in the standards:

- An extraordinary debate indicates that you can read a wide range of materials and build an understanding of the information, the cultures of the United States and other countries, and your place in this picture.

- To engage in an extraordinary debate, you must conduct research that shows your ability to gather information, evaluate it, and synthesize it into a form that supports your viewpoint.

- The speaking skills that you demonstrate in an extraordinary debate show that you know how to communicate effectively with a variety of audiences and for different purposes.

- Participation in an extraordinary debate demonstrates that you know how to use language to exchange information with others and to persuade others to adopt your viewpoint.

So Here's the Scoop

The way you are graded on a debate will vary, depending on what kind of debate you are doing and what kind of tournament and judge you have. When your teachers grade your in-class debate, they will do so based on a number of different educational standards.

Research: Was enough research done to support the argument? Was the research credible information from a variety of sources?

Arguments: Were they complex? Were they supported thoroughly with evidence and examples? Was the information logical? Was it up-to-date? Did emotions override facts?

Rebuttals: Did they address every point made by the opposition? Did they provide counterevidence?

Teamwork: Did each member of the team present an argument? Was there unity among the participants? Was everyone working together for a common goal? Did all team members avoid repetition and overlap of facts and evidence? Did members listen politely to each other, as well as to each person on the opposing team?

Behavior: Did students have a professional attitude? Did they show good manners? Did they dress and behave appropriately?

Speaking: Were students loud enough or quiet enough? Were speeches clear and easy to follow? Did students use facial expressions, gestures, and eye contact? Did each person stay within the allotted time limits?

What's a Debate Anyway?

Taking different sides of an issue and discussing it has been a human pastime for countless centuries. A debate is just another type of argument, but it is not a confrontation or a fight. It is not an emotional and distressful quarrel over distressing topics. **Instead, a debate is a structured, controlled, and judged contest between two sides taking opposing positions on the same topic.** In other words, this is not the same thing as the dispute you have with your sister over whose turn it is to drive the car to school. It is not personal; it is a way to examine an issue clearly and logically from both sides. If you lose, you may not like it or you may not get the grade you wanted, but you will not be emotionally devastated over it. (If you are, you took the assignment a little too seriously.)

"Debate provides a formal method for allowing [a] clash of ideas."

—Malcolm Kushner, author of *Public Speaking for Dummies*

Elements of the Debate

Talking

Debates are a type of public speaking, yet they are very different from a typical speech. They do, however, share some of the same qualities. Both require that you:

- **Speak clearly and confidently.**

- **Know your audience.**

- **Use good enunciation, projection, and presence.**

They also have a number of differences:

- **In a traditional speech, you speak slowly; in debate, you speak as quickly as possible while maintaining clarity.**

- **Body language is more subdued in debates than in traditional speeches.**

- **Speeches often teach or amuse; the goal of debate is to persuade and convince.**

Thinking Big

Debate also teaches you skills that go way beyond education. Debate keeps you current on world events, develops your sense of citizenship and ethics, points out any possible biases you might have, and helps you to analytically form some of your core values.

Shining

Why do students get involved in debate?

- **To compete and excel.** Perhaps you are not an athlete or a straight-A student. In debate you have the opportunity to grow and succeed—and even win trophies if you get involved in interscholastic debate competitions—just like the students who might stand out in sports or core academics.

- **For enjoyment.** Although it might be hard to imagine right now, there are also a number of students who choose to debate because it is enjoyable.

"You can always tell the debaters who enjoy debating from the ones that are forced to compete."

—Christine Pham, debate coach in Washington, D.C.

Overcoming

Surprisingly enough, some of the students who originally get involved in debate do so for a reason that you might know quite well: they are very, very shy. They hope that debate will help them overcome this trait as they attempt to "face their fears." Ben Garcia, half of the team that won the 2002 National Championship at the National Parliamentary Debate Association (NPDA) Tournament in Denver, Colorado, and now a law student, says, "I was so uncomfortable in front of people and I wanted to conquer that fear somehow." Sara Brueck Nichols, a debater who now works in marketing and sales, says, "I owe where I am today to participating in debate. I joined the debate team in my freshman year because I was incredibly shy but I wanted to be a journalist. My mom said, 'Are you crazy?' But debate helped me to overcome my fear of confrontation and taught me to be both well-spoken and well-written." Christi Siver, a coach of parliamentary debate at the University of Washington, says, "Debate gave me confidence because I was a really awkward teen."

TIP FILE

If you are shy, when you debate you can take on the persona of someone else, like an actor does when he goes onstage.

Thinking Ahead

Students who enjoy debates have gone into **education** (try disagreeing with a teacher if you are curious about his or her debating skills), **politics** (have you ever watched a presidential debate?), **broadcasting** (think of television or radio news and sports shows), **business** (have you ever heard a good sales pitch?), and even **religion** (think priest, rabbi, minister, or any other religious leader). Each of these fields calls for the very skills that debate teaches so well.

Gotta Learn the Lingo

Although the processes, time periods, and topics will depend on what style of debate you are engaging in, most debates share the same terminology. Take a minute to get familiar with these terms so that in the project chapters, it will be easier to follow along.

Affirmative:

This is one side of the debate. The affirmative side must convince the audience that:

1 Hey, there is a problem.

2 The current policy or system does not address the problem.

3 We have a plan to make things better.

For example, the affirmative side might say:

1 There is a problem with drugs in our school.

2 The current security system is not taking care of this problem.

3 We have a plan (police dogs, locker searches, and mandatory urine tests) that will make things much better.

The affirmative side is often fighting for CHANGE and this can be very challenging.

Negative:

This is the other side of the debate. The negative side must convince the audience that:

1 The affirmative side's plan will make things worse instead of better.

2 The plan does not address the real problem.

3 The current system is the best way to handle things OR that our counterplan is even better.

Constructive speech:

This is the first speech made by each side. In this speech, each side states its position on the resolution or statement.

Evidence:

Facts, examples, and statements from authorities used to strengthen your argument are called evidence.

Fallacies:

Errors in reasoning or arguments are fallacies.

Rebuttal:

This is the period in a debate when you refute the arguments made by your opponent. In other words, it is your chance to say (NOT in these terms): HEY! Your argument is wrong and mine is still right, and here is why!

Resolution:

This is a clear statement of what you are going to be debating. It is sometimes also known as the proposition or topic.

Heads Up!

So Here's the Scoop

So what's up with the word *forensic* in debate anyway?

Isn't that dealing with DNA, morgues, and scientific clues? Yes, generally forensic is associated with crime labs. But it is also a word that describes the process of engaging in public discussion or debate. Keep this in mind if you are researching debate online. Adding forensic to the search box can get you to some great links—as well as to some that tell you how to analyze evidence at a crime scene!

"Deliberation and debate is the way you stir the soul of our democracy."

—Jesse Jackson
(1941–   )

something you feel

headlines

Policy Resolution

Philosophical question

Lincoln-Douglas Deb

government and

headlines

20

foreign affai

HUNT AND GATHER

Finding Your Debate Topic

Finding Your Debate Topic

When you start to write a paper or prepare a speech, you have to begin with an idea. The same is true with a debate. This chapter will give you some clues about how to find the right idea that fits everything from your interests and the grading criteria to your teacher's requirements. You will learn about the basic kinds of debates including policy resolution, Lincoln-Douglas, and in-class debates. You will also be introduced to the model debate we will be exploring throughout the next few chapters.

The process of finding a topic to debate is somewhat different from selecting an essay or a speech topic. With certain types of debates, you do not get a choice. The resolution that you will research and speak on is already decided and given to you. Your focus, then, is on understanding and researching the topic provided. With a **policy resolution debate**, for example, the proposition is announced once a year and that topic is what all debate teams work on. In **Lincoln-Douglas debates**, the proposition changes every couple of months. With **in-class debates**, the teacher may either provide you with the idea or ask you to come up with your own. In the following pages you will find lots of ideas to choose from, and you will find out how to know if an idea is worth debating.

Policy Resolution Debate

In policy resolution debate, the topics usually revolve around current events within government. They are very complex topics, and they warrant a great deal of research and study. Some examples from recent years include resolutions on nuclear bans, financial aid to foreign countries, and issues surrounding the use of energy resources.

Lincoln-Douglas Debate

At the high school level, Lincoln-Douglas debates are about arguing basic values or ethics rather than governmental policies. Many of them come straight from current newspaper headlines. These topics change every two months. This gives debaters time to learn and study, but not at the in-depth level of the policy resolution debate. Many of the ideas fall under the categories of:

- **Individual versus Society** (me and you versus everyone else)

- **Government and Law** (how they affect people's lives)

- **Foreign Affairs** (relationships with other parts of the world)

- **Economics** (the world of money and business)

- **Environment** (what is the condition of the planet and how to affect it)

- **Bioethics** (what is right or wrong in the practice of science)

- **Education** (issues about learning)

- **Gender** (male/female issues)

- **Philosophical Questions** (deep thoughts to ponder)

"It is better to debate a question without settling it than to settle a question without debating it."

—Joseph Joubert, eighteenth-century French philosopher

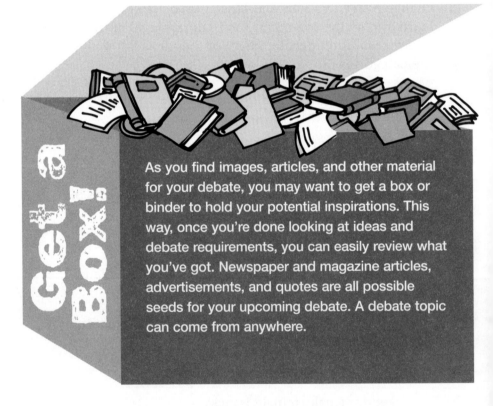

Get a Box!

As you find images, articles, and other material for your debate, you may want to get a box or binder to hold your potential inspirations. This way, once you're done looking at ideas and debate requirements, you can easily review what you've got. Newspaper and magazine articles, advertisements, and quotes are all possible seeds for your upcoming debate. A debate topic can come from anywhere.

In-Class Debate

In-class debates can be in any format that your teacher chooses. They are often quite different from policy resolution debates or Lincoln-Douglas debates. Perhaps your teacher has already assigned you a topic. If so, you have your starting point. Perhaps a list of possibilities was provided. If so, you have to make a choice. Maybe you have been asked to come up with an idea all on your own. Don't panic. It's not so hard. Here are some points to mull over.

Your first focus should be on how to know if an idea is worth debating.

Look at some of the potential topics:

- Should cell phones be allowed in classrooms?

- Should hunting be banned as a sport?

- Should teen criminals be locked up in adult prisons?

- Should the government institute a rating system for popular music?

- Should students go to school year-round?

- Should skateboarding be banned in public places?

- Should school newspapers be censored?

- Should schools have dress codes?

- Should teens have part-time jobs while they are in school?

- Should there be a limit on how much homework is assigned per class?

- Should the government raise or lower the age to smoke, drink, drive, or vote?

Is It Debatable?

Did you see a topic that you liked? Or did any of them inspire you to come up with your own idea? If so, take your idea and put it through the following questions:

1 Can you think of arguments for both sides of the issue, even if you only agree with one side? Are you able to "walk in another person's shoes," as they say?

2 Is this a hot topic? Are people talking about it? Have you watched news programs about it on television? Have you read newspaper headlines about it? Is it on the magazine covers in the grocery store?

3 Is this a question that you have thought or talked about in the past? Have you stayed awake at night pondering it? Have you discussed it in the cafeteria or with a friend at a sleepover?

4 Do you have a strong, emotional reaction to the idea? Does it make you feel furious, frustrated, frantic, or fantastic?

5 Do you know others who would have a strong, emotional reaction to it (regardless of whether they agreed or disagreed with your viewpoint)? Would it make your mom grind her teeth, your dad jump up on a soapbox, or your friend start pacing back and forth in the locker room?

6 Is this an idea that you think will have a lot of related resource materials? Will you be able to access information about this topic at the library? Are there Web sites and magazine articles about it? Is there a *60 Minutes* segment dedicated just to this issue?

The more questions that you respond to with a yes, the more likely it is that you have come up with a good debate topic.

Your research, preparation, and performance will all be enhanced if you have a personal interest—or even a passion—for the subject. If the thought of eating meat is repulsive, choose something to do with vegetarianism. If the idea of legally restricting what you can read or look at makes your skin crawl, choose censorship. Your enthusiasm will shine through to your audience, your partner, your teacher, and your judge. It will bring an ordinary debate much closer to being an extraordinary one.

It all begins with   Without it, you are stuck in the beginning with nowhere to go. For our model, we need a topic that fits all the requirements of an in-class debate and has the potential to be extraordinary. To show you how to do it, let's focus on this topic:

Run this topic through the questions on page 26.

Have an opinion already?

Can you see both sides of the issue?

Feel your heart beating faster now?

Will there be resources available to help you research this topic?

Okay then, let's go! It's time to find out where to get the best information, how to know it's the good stuff, and how to put it all together in the right order.

PROJECT JUMP START

If you need some extra resources for your debate, check out these Web sites:

For policy resolution debate topics dating back to 1946:
http://www.wfu.edu/organizations/NDT/ HistoricalLists/topics.html

For Lincoln-Douglas debate topics:
http://cas.bethel.edu/dept/comm/nfa/nfa-ld.html

For in-class debate topics, some pretty hot and controversial topics can be found at:
http://facstaff.bloomu.edu/jtomlins/debate_ topics.htm; or http://www.multcolib.org /homework/sochc.html; or http://kiwiyert.tripod.com/ideas_ for_debate_topics.htm.

HIT THE BOOKS

At the library, get a hold of *100 Hot Debate Topics for Your Classes* by **Allison Buza** (Teacher's Discovery, 1999) or *Speak Out! Debate and Public Speaking in the Middle Grades* by John Meany and Kate Shuster (International Debate Education Association, 2005).

BRAIN JAM:
Prep for an Interview

Scan the headlines. Pick up a variety of newspapers—school, city, national, or international—and line them up. Are there any topics they have in common? What seems to be on people's minds, no matter where they live? Look for trends and write them down. When you're done, read the list and see which ideas excite you.

Knock on some classroom doors. Ask some teachers if you can come in and ask a question. If they agree, ask them what concerns teachers have today. How do those concerns affect students? Can you focus on their worries and students' perspectives and come up with a debate topic? You could also request permission to visit a parent-teacher association or faculty meeting to ask your questions.

Strike up a conversation with your local librarians. Ask what trends they have seen in recent book titles. What topics seem to be lighting fires under patrons? Which books can't be kept on the shelves? What titles do patrons call and request? Which one of these can be turned into a debate topic?

winning debate

Pare it dow

Strong opini

quality of evidence

Fa

in-depth research

testimonials

Press R

quality and quantity

Af

30

Pare it down

THE VISION

Researching Your Debate

Researching Your Debate

One look at the lists of debate ideas from the previous chapter should be enough to bring home an important point about the process: *It takes research.* In this chapter, we will look at:

- **how much research you need;**
- **what kind of research you need;**
- **where to find the research you need;**
- **how to recognize quality research;**
- **what sources are best;**
- **how to keep your information organized and clear.**

How Much Do I Have to Do?

Even if you have a strong opinion about the topic you are going to debate, it is not enough to just go with that alone—especially because you may not be arguing on the side you agree with! **A winning debate is one that is based on solid, up-to-date, and authoritative research.** Anything less is disappointing and frustrating for all involved.

First, let's look at how much of it you have to do. It simply depends on the depth and breadth of your topic. For your topic on whether or not music negatively affects teenagers, for example, you will need to do some research—but it will most likely be quite a bit less than if you were debating alternative energy sources for the United States. It is, however, no less important to do your research well.

"When both sides have good arguments, the quality of one's evidence is what elevates you above your opponent."

—Shawn Whalen, Director of Speech and Debate at San Francisco State University

Policy debates usually require the most in-depth research. They are centered on global issues that have many points of view, statistics, facts, and other elements that you have to know about. **Lincoln-Douglas** and **parliamentary debates** also require a lot of research into politics and procedure. **In-class debates** are different from these when it comes to research. Does this mean you are off the hook and don't have to spend much time researching? **NO**. Read that again. **NO**. An in-class debate requires research, too—just a different kind. Instead of looking through government documentation, meeting minutes, and policy changes, you will focus more on recent trends, media headlines, and school textbooks. The research you do for your in-class debate is just as vital to its success as the research for any other

TIP FILE

If you want to win your debate, don't just research your side of the issue. Research the **other side** of the issue as well so that you can anticipate their points and arguments and have rebuttal information prepared; have a deeper understanding of the key issues within the topic; know the other side's weakest points; and see any potential holes in your arguments.

type of debate. Most likely, your teacher will thoroughly discuss with you what research is expected for the project. If that doesn't happen, start asking questions.

What kind of information are you looking for?
You want to find anything that supports your side of the debate. This will include:

- reasons
- facts
- studies
- research results
- testimonies
- reports
- press releases
- statements

plus details from organizations, agencies, and individuals. (In short: find everything you possibly can.)

Where Am I Going to Find This Info?

Many debate coaches and teachers around the country remember a time when ALL research was done with only magazines, newspapers, and books. They had to read and clip articles and quotes and then actually take them to an ancient copy machine so that every person on the team could have a copy to refer to and cite. Today, those sources are still used, but the Internet is also a huge presence in research.

As you probably already know from researching other topics on the Internet, some sites are wonderful resources and others are frighteningly unreliable. You need to make sure you are using the gold mines and not the land mines. "The Net is good, but most likely the first twenty hits on Google are not going to be great," says Joe Patrice, a former debater and now a lawyer in New York. "With research, it is not just knowing where to go; it's the ability to discern what is good material and what is not."

Surfing the Net

When it comes to online searching, you can start with the biggest search engines. The largest sites are (in this order):

- **Google**
- **Yahoo!**
- **MSN Search**
- **AOL Search**
- **Terra Lycos**
- **AltaVista**
- **Ask Jeeves**

These search engines often can only provide general information. You will get a mix of the good, the bad, and the ridiculous. If you simply put "music teenagers" in the search box, you will get more hits than you will know what to do with—and most of them will not be helpful at all. Refine your search by trying a combination of words, such as "music harmful teens" or "music damaging teenagers" or even "music affects teenagers."

TIP FILE

Find a mentor at your school or in your community whom you can bounce ideas off of and practice arguments with and who can offer advice from his or her perspective.

Heads Up!

So Here's the Scoop

Many times, your arguments will be based on stories that are currently or were recently in the news. Some good news sites include:

AlltheWeb News: *http://www.alltheweb.com/?cat=news*

AltaVista News: *http://news.altavista.com*

Ananova: *http://www.ananova.com*

Columbia Newsblaster: *http://www1.cs.columbia.edu/nlp/newsblaster*

DailyEarth.com: *http://dailyearth.com*

Daypop: *http://www.daypop.com*

Google News: *http://news.google.com*

HeadlineSpot: *http://www.headlinespot.com*

Kiosken: *http://www.esperanto.se/kiosk/engindex.html*

NewsDirectory: *http://www.newsdirectory.com*

RocketNews: *http://www.rocketnews.com*

WorldNews Network: *http://www.wn.com*

Yahoo! News: *http://news.yahoo.com*

To search magazines and other periodicals for past articles, try these Web sites:

FindArticles: *http://www.findarticles.com*

MagPortal: *http://www.magportal.com*

In addition to the Net, magazines, newspapers, and books, other useful sources are previous debates on the same topic, official government documents, and speech transcripts. Some recommended resources are:

Associated Press Wire Services

Christian Science Monitor

CNN Headline News

CNN Newsroom

National Public Radio

New York Times

USA Today

"Great debaters have an arsenal of information in their heads, which makes for lively and very interesting debate rounds."

—Christine Pham, debate coach

A Look at Our Sample Debate

Thirty minutes of searching properly on the Net should yield some good places to start reading about the effect of music on teenagers. Remember to look at both sides of the issue for additional information.

Here are some questions to consider on this topic:

- How does music affect people of all ages? Good, bad, not at all?

- How does it affect teenagers specifically? Any differences?

- Do different kinds of music have different effects? Does classical make us smarter and hard rock make us more violent?

- How do lyrics affect listeners? What has more impact—the music or the lyrics?

- Can the noise level of the music be harmful?

- How does music affect our studying skills? Listening skills? Driving skills?

- Does music intensify or dilute our emotions?

- What part do music videos play in this issue?

- How does music affect other living creatures and is this significant?

Keeping It All Together

Once you have started your research, how do you keep it organized? Just as with a research paper, you can keep the information on one side of multiple 4-by-6-inch index cards.

1 **Put the name of the argument at the top of each card and then write down all of the supporting evidence you find on it.** Numbering the cards is a good idea so that in case you drop them, life does not come to a crashing end while you try to figure out how to put the cards back in the proper order. Note cards are usually better than spiral notebooks because when you are debating, you want the air to be filled with the anticipation of your next statement, not the sound of flipping pages.

2 **In the beginning, you may want to write down most information word-for-word,** especially your opening and closing statements.

3 **As you practice your speech, however, you can begin to pare it down** (other than quotes, which should always be written out completely and marked clearly with quotation marks). Keep chipping away until your paragraphs become sentences, your sentences become phrases, and your phrases become words.

The Process

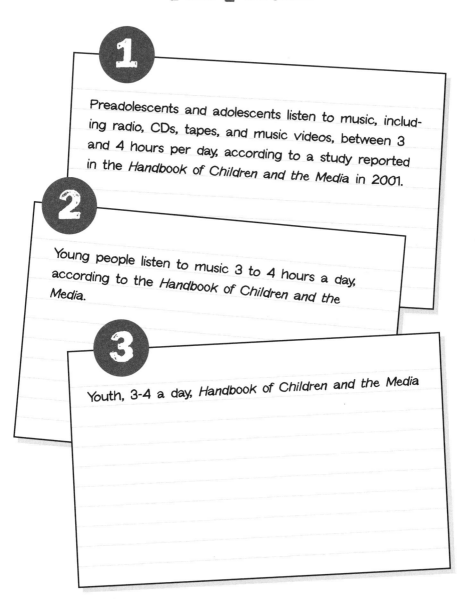

1

Preadolescents and adolescents listen to music, including radio, CDs, tapes, and music videos, between 3 and 4 hours per day, according to a study reported in the *Handbook of Children and the Media* in 2001.

2

Young people listen to music 3 to 4 hours a day, according to the *Handbook of Children and the Media*.

3

Youth, 3-4 a day, *Handbook of Children and the Media*

As you practice and become more familiar with the material, it will get easier.

Make sure that you develop a system for referencing where the information you are referring to came from. You can use different colors of ink for each source or create a code for each. For example, the statistic above came from a study reported in the ***Handbook of Children and the Media,*** published by Sage Publications in 2001. You could write HCM/SP/01. Feel free to create whatever system works best for you—just remember how to decode it!

Finding enough information is usually not the hardest part of researching. Instead, the hardest part is finding too much and having to choose what to use and what not to use. You have to read, think, and weigh the impact of your information. You must compare all the pieces of information and reject the ones that are not strong enough.

Finding the Good Stuff

How do you know what order to put the research in? What qualifies as the "good stuff"? Here are some questions to ask that will clarify the process:

* **Did you say "Wow!" or "Really?" or "You're kidding!" when you read it?** If so, there's an excellent chance it was an important point to include.

* **Did you find perspectives that you had not thought of before?** If so, keep them in mind as you develop your arguments.

* **Where did the information come from?** If it's from an educational or government site, give it more importance than www.kidswholistentorap.com.

* **Are there numbers involved?** Often the most powerful information includes some kind of statistic. Lead with the strong stats from the best sources.

* **Can you see holes in the argument or point of view?** Chances are, if you can, your opponents certainly will. Can you find the information you need to respond to challenges to your argument? If not, this might not be the best point to bring up.

Quality and quantity of research is important in winning a debate. Spend the time you should on it. You never know when you will come across a tiny morsel of information that your opponent will surely miss that will end up making your debate extraordinary.

HELPFUL RESOURCES

Another helpful Web site to check out for current research is High Beam Research at *http://www.highbeam.com/library/index.asp.* It includes 34 million articles from three thousand different sources. For law information, as well as public records and government information, go to LexisNexis at *http://www.lexisnexis.com/.* Most public libraries subscribe to large informational databases, so be sure to check with your school, public, and university librarians for recommended sources.

TIP FILE

Want to make sure you are getting your information from a high-quality source? Go to Google and click on "Advanced Search." Once you are there, put your search words in and then indicate you only want sites that end in .edu (education), .org (organizations), or .gov (government) to come up. These sites may not be perfect, but they weed out the ones trying to sell you something along with blogs, personal opinions, and more.

BRAIN JAM:
Developing Your Topic

Throw it out there. Take your debate idea and throw it out for discussion with your family, friends, and classmates. What opinions do people have about it? What perspectives do they bring up that you hadn't even thought about before? What new angles could you use for your argument based on their thoughts and comments? Don't just ask people your own age. Ask your parents. Ask your grandparents or people their age. Ask little kids. See how the different generations have varying perspectives on the topic.

Know the territory. Pick a random topic that you find interesting. Give yourself thirty minutes and hit the keyboard. How many Web sites can you come up with that look viable? Check out the library site for book titles. Hit some of the sites listed earlier for possible magazine articles on the topic. When thirty minutes is up, see how many sites you have. Spending time doing this gives you tips, clues, and practice for researching the real topic and speeds up the process.

Burden of proof

typical for

Common fallacie

rguing for the affirmativ

opening stateme

Rebuttal st

Common

Fallacy

burden of pro

THINK OUT OF THE BOX

If Point A Leads to Point B

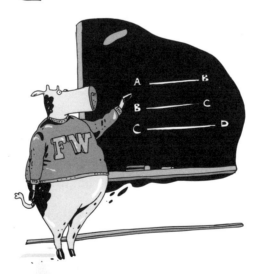

If Point A Leads to Point B

In the world of debate, everything revolves around the argument. In this chapter, you will learn how to:

- **argue for the affirmative side;**
- **argue for the negative side;**
- **deal with the intense phase of the rebuttal argument;**
- **avoid the most common argument mistakes;**
- **create a flow sheet.**

Although the different types of debates have different requirements, with an in-class debate, you will be taking one side of an issue or another. Whichever side you are on, you will only win through a strong and powerful argument. Think of your argument as a superhero. It can't be injured, ignored, or ruined.

Arguing for the Affirmative

If you are on the affirmative side of a debate, the biggest burden of proof is on you. You speak first and have to make a strong impression in your constructive speech. To do this well, you have to show that the issue is significant. You must identify the issue and then show why you believe the answer to it is affirmative, or YES.

In our model debate, for example, you will have to state that **YES, music DOES negatively affect teenagers.** To support this (instead of just relying on your own personal opinion), you need statistics, quotes, and examples supporting your position. You may get a chance to do a second constructive speech, but in most in-class debates, there is only one per side.

TIP FILE

Using quotes in your arguments is often a good idea. You can either state them word for word or paraphrase (summarize) them. Quoting them verbatim is usually best if the quote is brief (one hundred words or less). Remember, your time is limited so you must use every second wisely.

Arguing for the Negative

If you are arguing for the negative, it will be your job to take the opposite viewpoint on the issue in your constructive speech. In this case, you would be saying **NO, music does not negatively affect teenagers.** You want to prove this through making new points and responding with different angles and information.

Sample Opening Statements

Look at these examples. When you read the ordinary ones, do you find yourself yawning and saying, yeah, so what? What happens when you read the extraordinary ones? They are much more interesting and have a solid foundation in fact.

ORDINARY	EXTRAORDINARY
(Affirmative side) Teenagers really like music, and they listen to it quite often during the course of a typical day, which may cause some problems for them.	(Affirmative side) According to recent studies reported in professional literature, teenagers listen to music more than they watch television, listen to the radio, or read books, and it is not doing them any good in the process.
(Negative side) There are many wonderful things about music, and it is no surprise that it plays a big part in teen culture.	(Negative side) Listening to music calms people, enhances learning, entertains people of all ages, and even helps us to stay healthier.

After your opening statements, each team presents its arguments. This is where you list those numbers, studies, reports, and stories. If you were on the affirmative side, for example, you might include:

Affirmative Arguments

- Many popular song lyrics support the ideas of violence, suicide, the occult, and the devaluation of women.

- In a report from the Driving Organization, listening to loud music in the car can delay your reaction time enough to put you and others in potential danger.

- According to a Gallup poll, 59 percent of Americans would like to see restrictions in the amount of violent content allowed in music.

If you were on the negative side, you might include:

Negative Arguments

- In one recent study reported at the Intel International Science and Engineering Fair, it was shown that listening to music for twenty minutes a day for six weeks can cause your body to produce more white blood cells than average.

- Medical studies have recently shown that music has a healing effect on people and is increasingly being used in hospital rooms and operating rooms.

- Multiple studies released under the umbrella title of "The Mozart Effect" show how music improves the brain's abstract reasoning skills.

- Many teachers use music in the classroom to help students imagine, create, and relax.

Can You Feel the Heat?

When the negative side is done with the constructive speech, they get to go directly into the **rebuttal,** often referred to as the "pressure cooker" portion of the debate. This is when things get more intense and the competitive spirit climbs. **For both sides, the rebuttal phase involves attacking the other side's evidence and the quality of their sources.** This is where you will find out if you have made any mistakes.

The rebuttal portion of a debate is where things get more passionate. Both sides have made their initial arguments and now comes the time to say, here is why you are wrong and I am right. (Saying "nah-nah-nah-nah-nah" is not allowed, however.) **Now you are not just defining your position, you are defending it.** To increase the tension, the time you have for rebuttal is much shorter, so the pressure is certainly on! You had better know what you are going to do so you don't waste those precious seconds.

The rebuttal is virtually the same, regardless of the type of debate.

The Rebuttal

- provides a brief (usually sixty seconds or less) overview of what has been mentioned in earlier arguments;

- recaps the main points—but be sure to slant or frame them in your favor, if possible;

- demonstrates your "road map"—a virtual map that shows you where you are going from here and shows the judge and your audience your pattern of organization;

- gives you the chance to defend your arguments against the opposition's statements;

- attacks the opposition's points;

- gives you the chance to expand and reinforce your previous arguments;

- allows you the time to destroy or deny the opponent's arguments by attacking the value of their evidence and the soundness of their reasoning.

TIP FILE

If you lose a tournament because of poor argumentation, a weak rebuttal, or botched delivery, practice it again afterward the way you wish you had done it.

Sample Rebuttal Statements

What makes a rebuttal statement extraordinary? Take a look at these examples.

ORDINARY	EXTRAORDINARY
(Affirmative side) It just is not true that putting warning labels on compact discs is enough to keep kids from buying music with violent and sexual lyrics.	(Affirmative side) The opponent said that putting black and white warning labels on compact discs was enough to keep kids from buying music with violent or sexual lyrics, but that is not correct. While these labels have been applied since 1990 to meet congressional demands, the requirement is optional, so many recording companies do not cooperate. And because the label is on the outside of the packaging only, it is easily discarded before parents even see it.
(Negative side) The other team pointed out that music helps us to learn, but learn what?	(Negative side) The opponent showed statistics that proved children learned new material quickly and easily when it was put to music. But doesn't this mean that if the lyrics are advocating violence, drug and alcohol use, and other dangerous habits that listeners will learn that information more quickly and easily also?

TYPICAL FORMAT FOR DEBATES

Rules

ALL debates have two (or more) sides.

ALL debates begin with a constructive speech.

ALL debates contain some kind of rebuttal.

BOTH sides must have an equal number of speakers.

BOTH sides must have an equal, limited amount of time to speak.

Affirmative team usually speaks first and last.

Although the amount of time and the order for speaking can vary from one type of debate to another, here is a typical format:

First constructive speech by AFFIRMATIVE team	☞	**10 minutes**
First constructive speech by the NEGATIVE team	☞	**10 minutes**
Second constructive speech by the AFFIRMATIVE team	☞	**10 minutes**
Second constructive speech by the NEGATIVE team	☞	**10 minutes**
First rebuttal by NEGATIVE team	☞	**5 minutes**
First rebuttal by AFFIRMATIVE team	☞	**5 minutes**
Second rebuttal by NEGATIVE team	☞	**5 minutes**
Second rebuttal by AFFIRMATIVE team	☞	**5 minutes**

The Most Common Fallacies or Mistakes

It is easy to make mistakes when you are putting together your argument. When you see the word *fallacy* in the debating world, just think mistake, error, blunder, blooper, flub, slipup—you get the idea. Here are the most common ones. If you make them, your debate plummets a long way from extraordinary and winds up much closer to disappointing.

Avoid the following:

1. **Quoting someone or using a statistic without stating where it came from.** By saying, "According to the National Institutes of Health's Teen Media study, 40 percent of the music teens listen to focuses on sex and relationships," you will have a lot more credibility than just throwing out the statistic on its own. **When you cite a source, however, make sure it is SOLID.** It must be a reliable and competent one. In other words, if you are quoting tax law and you mention a specific paragraph in a form from the Internal Revenue Service, you have authority. If you quote your Uncle Bill, who has been doing taxes for years, you don't.

2. **Bad manners. Always respect your opponents.** For example, in your music debate, if your opponent has never taken music lessons and you have, and you said, "Well, of course SHE wouldn't know anything about classical music," this is a fallacy. It makes the debate personal, instead of professional, and loses you points (and friends!).

3. **Inconsistency. You have to stick by what you say.** If you quoted a statistic or told a story, don't use another one later in your arguments that directly contradicts it. **Be consistent in your arguments at all times.**

4 **Irrelevancy.** **Only use relevant data for your argument** or else you are making an error called introducing a red herring. This is the verbal equivalent of pointing at something behind someone's shoulder and then stealing their dessert while they are not looking. A red herring is irrelevant information used to distract your opponent. If you say, for example, that you heard your opponent listening to a satanic song by Marilyn Manson, you may distract him so much that he cannot respond appropriately. This may be effective, but it is sneaky and considered bad manners.

5 **Not keeping current.** **Make sure your statistics and stories are up-to-date.** You do not want to lose because you quoted a study done twenty years ago. Your opponent will easily spot it and say that those facts are no longer reliable.

6 **Silly examples.** **Use examples that are truly representative of your argument.** In other words, to support your argument that music affects teenagers negatively, don't state that one kid went out and hurt someone after listening to a Led Zeppelin tune. It is such a rare example that the opposing side will easily strike down the argument. (Now if 82 percent of the people who listened to Led Zeppelin went out and committed a crime, you would have a fact to use.)

How can you possibly keep track of all the different arguments and points made by your team and your opponent? Many debaters use a form called a flow sheet. This is where each team records the arguments, counterarguments, and evidence for both sides. Usually debaters create their own system of shorthand to do this efficiently and quickly. You can use abbreviations and leave out adjectives, conjunctions (and, for, but, so), helping verbs (is, will, have), or articles (a, an, the). The flow sheet saves you time and keeps you more organized. A legal-sized notepad divided into four sections is the most common format to use. It usually looks something like the sample on the next page.

TIP FILE

Too often we stop thinking outside the realm of the familiar, and in debating, this will cause you a lot of trouble. When you think of something, or someone suggests something, and your immediate reaction is, "That's not possible," question it. Often an extremely strong argument is hiding just outside where you normally stop thinking.

FLOW SHEET

Affirmative Case	Outline of team's case (words/phrases). *Listen a lot—too much? and causes problems.*
Negative Case	Opposing team's main points and evidence. *calms, enhances, entertains, and healthier?*
Affirmative Counterargument	Arguments or evidence to use in the rebuttal. *violence, suicide, occult, women, driving res., rap/arrest, poll 4 restriction*
Negative Counterargument	Counterarguments by opposition side's rebuttal. *more WBC, hospitals, Mozart, classroom use*

59

PROJECT JUMP START

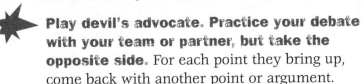

★ **Make a list of the main points you want to cover in your debate.** Next to them, write all the arguments you can think of that your opponent might make. Ask your family and friends to think of some additional ones. Once you have a good list, look through your research and find statistics that you can use to rebut each point.

★ **Play devil's advocate. Practice your debate with your team or partner, but take the opposite side.** For each point they bring up, come back with another point or argument. This will help you to spot holes in your argument that you might have missed.

BRAIN JAM:
At the Movies

Rent some courtroom dramas. No one debates better than a lawyer—especially in movies. Rent some films that center on a courtroom trial and watch the lawyers. How do they bring up points? How do they support them? Here are a few oldies but goodies to start with. Yeah, they're in black and white, but they're worth it!

12 Angry Men

Anatomy of a Murder

The Caine Mutiny

Inherit the Wind

To Kill a Mockingbird

Witness for the Prosecution

practice, practice

Negative

Your words show emo

Practice,
Practice,
Practice

Tone

SP

body langu

Ne

Breathe

Enunciate

THE SPIN ROOM

Speak Now or Forever Hold Your Peace

Speak Now or Forever Hold Your Peace

Once you have your topic and your research, it's time to focus on what you need to do to give a strong speech. In this chapter, you will learn about:

- **the importance of practice;**

- **keeping eye contact with your audience;**

- **knowing what your body is saying that your mouth isn't;**

- **the skills of breathing and enunciating;**

- **how to monitor your volume and tone.**

There is a saying that the only thing people fear more than public speaking is death. While it may not be that dire or dramatic for you, the concept of standing up in front of people and not only speaking but arguing may seem a bit intimidating. The way to get around that fear (and bypass ordinary for extraordinary in the process) is to **learn how to speak with confidence.** It can be done, but it takes a number of different factors to pull it off. Here are some quick tips for making the experience a positive and successful one.

Know Your Stuff

The number-one way to ensure that your speech goes well is knowing your material inside out. The more confident you are in your evidence and arguments, the more assertively you will present them. A lot of insecurity can come from wondering if you have the best facts, enough data, and strong points. If you have researched thoroughly and practiced regularly, your preparation will shine through.

Pronunciation

Make sure you know how to pronounce all of the terms you use in your debate. There might be foreign words or technical terms, and you have to be comfortable using them. You will lose credibility immediately if you pronounce a vital term incorrectly.

Make Eye Contact

You may want to keep your eyes plastered to your notes, but you will make more of a connection with your audience—your teacher and classmates—if you make an effort to look directly at them. **Eye contact implies confidence and establishes rapport between you and your listeners.**

Strike an even balance when looking at someone directly. If you avoid looking at someone, you will come across as dishonest or uncomfortable. If you look into someone's eyes for too long without looking away, it can appear to be an aggressive challenge. So look at your audience just long enough to connect with them.

Know Your Weaknesses

As you practice your speech in front of the mirror, into a tape or video recorder, or to your family and friends, note your weaknesses. Do you pause too long between points? Do you fill up space with ahs, ums, and you knows? Do you stumble over your words? Do you speak too loudly or too quietly? Do you mumble? The first step to improving those weaknesses is to identify them. Check out the exercises on pages 70–75 to help you with many of those issues.

Be Aware of Body Language and Appearance

If you can, videotape yourself doing a presentation. Turn off the sound so that you can concentrate on just your physical presence. Are you standing up straight? Do you use natural gestures? Is your face animated? Avoid wearing noisy jewelry or distracting colors when you speak. Make sure you don't flip a pen, play with your hair, or engage in any other annoying habit that may bug your audience and interfere with your message.

Practice, Practice, Practice

This cannot be emphasized enough. **The more you practice, the more you will know the material, improve your weaknesses, figure out spots that need work, and learn more about how to speak well.** Practice in front of your cereal bowl in the morning and before you go to bed at night. Show off to your friends. Dazzle your parents. Amaze your grandparents. Bore the dog. But practice!

Isn't This Just Like Making a Speech?

Although making a speech and participating in a debate have many things in common, they also have a few important differences. Perhaps the most striking one is that **you must learn to speak quickly, without losing any clarity.** (Think of pharmaceutical commercials on television that have mere seconds to list their 2.3 million negative side effects.) Your time in any debate is limited, usually ranging from two to ten minutes, and you have to use each one of those sixty-second segments wisely. Debaters often refer to this as using "word economy." You don't want to be repetitious or take up the teacher's time with anything other than important, well-presented material. Many of the drills that debate students learn focus on how to speak faster while remaining totally clear. Not an easy thing to do, especially if you throw a little anxiety into the mix.

TIP FILE

Engage the judge. Speak to the judge as if you were in a courtroom speaking to the jury. Impress him or her with your research, confidence, and style. This will give your teacher compelling reasons to give you that grade you're hoping to get.

Time to Drill (Fortunately, NOT at the Dentist)

Many people have some kind of speaking habit or style that can be troublesome when they start out. There are a number of drills out there to help you overcome them. They may sound a little odd, but they can be quite helpful.

1 **Breathing.** Because you are often speaking very quickly, it is easy to run out of air. Gasping rarely makes a good impression on a judge, a class, or an audience. Learning how to breathe from your diaphragm instead of your chest will help. (Just talk to someone in choir. Singers learn this early on!) **Make sure you are standing up straight and that you take a breath at the commas, semicolons, and periods in your notes.** If your voice tends to be too high, it is usually a combination of nerves and poor breathing techniques.

2 **Enunciation. Saying your words clearly is perhaps the most important element in any kind of public speaking.** If you have ever had the unfortunate experience of speaking to a telemarketer on the phone who does not speak clearly, you know what I mean. Can you imagine how quickly a teacher or a judge would give up on a debater who might have the best arguments in the world but cannot be understood?

To attack this problem, practice overenunciating. Say each ending consonant crisply. If you have ever sung in a choir or performed in a play, you know this lesson already. You may think you sound ridiculous, but by overdoing it, you are training your brain, lips, tongue, and mouth to say things very carefully.

There are many different tricks you can use to improve your enunciation. You can:

- Recite a song lyric or poem that you know well. Say the words clearly and hit the ending consonants firmly. Speed up as you improve.

- Practice your speech while holding a pen in your mouth.

- Read your speech backward. This will help you focus on enunciating rather than on the meaning of each word.

3 **Volume.** **If you tend to speak too loudly, whisper your entire presentation. If you tend to be too quiet, shout it.** One coach told a story of how one of her students spoke very quietly, primarily because he had a slight speech impediment. To help him speak louder, she had him practice reading to the other members of the debate team while a vacuum cleaner ran next to him. If they couldn't hear him over the vacuum, he had to start over again.

4 **Tone.** If you have ever seen the movie *Ferris Bueller's Day Off,* you may remember the teacher with the dreadful monotone (the well-known Ben Stein). Just as he was no fun at all to listen to, neither are you if you debate in a monotone. You will sound bored and probably bore your audience as well. **Make sure that your words show emotion—anger, sadness, delight, humor— where appropriate.**

If you are not sure of what tones you use, have someone tape-record or videotape one of your practice sessions. Listen carefully. To help make sure you emphasize important words in your arguments, you can highlight, circle, or underline them.

HIT THE BOOKS

If you want to learn more about effective public speaking, pick up a copy of *The Power of Speech* by Marie Stuttard (Barron's, 1997). It is full of practical tips on speech preparation and delivery.

TIP FILE

Have fun! No one wants to watch unhappy or uncomfortable debaters. If they enjoy the sport and showing off their research and their quick minds, they will have extraordinary debates. You can almost always tell the debaters who enjoy debating from the ones who are forced to compete.

PROJECT JUMP START

★ **Take a deep breath.**
To help you control your breathing, try this experiment. Hold a straight-back chair in front of you at chest height. Keep your arms as straight as possible. Put a paper to read on the seat. Read the paper aloud. Put the chair down and read it aloud again. Listen for the difference. You will be prevented from gasping while holding the chair.

You can also learn to control the speed at which you exhale, which will prevent gasping as well. One way to work on this is to take a deep breath and exhale as slowly as possible. Time it. Practice each day and see if you can do it slower and slower. You can also practice in front of a lit candle. If you exhale too fast, you will blow it out. If you do it nice and slowly, you will only make it flicker.

BRAIN JAM:
I Hear You Loud and Clear!

Twist your tongue: For extra practice on enunciation, read some tongue twisters aloud until you can do them without stumbling. Here are some to get you started:

Brisk, brave brigadiers brandished broad, bright blades, blunderbusses, and bludgeons—balancing them badly.

Suddenly swerving, seven small swans
Swam silently southward,
Seeing six swift sailboats
Sailing sedately seaward.

Pump up the volume: To practice making yourself heard, have family or friends take up three positions in a room: one person a few feet in front of you, another halfway across the room, and a third as far back as possible. Start your speech. Whenever you cannot be clearly heard they should raise their hands. That is your cue to talk louder. Repeat your speech several times and see if you can make it all the way through without any of them putting up their hands.

Ethics

Values

One-person team

opinions

Scoring

re

Structur

easoning

Tournaments

BEING CONVINCING

Lincoln-Douglas Debates

Lincoln-Douglas Debates

Let's look at one of the most common types of debates in classrooms and at tournaments. In this chapter, you will find out:

- **how the Lincoln-Douglas debates got their start;**
- **how the debates are structured and scored;**
- **what kind of ideas you can use for Lincoln-Douglas debates.**

The Lincoln-Douglas debates are based on debates held in 1858 between Abraham Lincoln and Stephen Douglas. Both men were campaigning for one of Illinois's two U.S. Senate seats, and although Douglas won, it was Lincoln who went on to become U.S. president. Their style of debating is the foundation of this format of debate, although things have come a long way in the last 150 years.

Lincoln-Douglas debates are held between two individuals instead of two two-member teams. They allow you to examine questions about values, opinions, and ethics. Each side is responsible for convincing the judge that its set of values is more important than the other side's. In this format:

- There is **less emphasis on research and evidence** and **more on reasoning and persuasion.**

- Participants are judged on who has the **best grasp of the issue,** who **best defends that premise,** and which side mounts the **strongest attack.**

- You are **judged more on how you use evidence** rather than on how much of it you use.

"The action of the body and voice in connection with the highest function of a rational being, communication of thought, must be considered one of the noblest and finest departments of physical activity."

—Solomon Clark, *Principles of Vocal Expression and Literary Interpretation*

What Are the Topics?

What kinds of topics are discussed in Lincoln-Douglas debates? Although they change with the times and often **focus on what is hot in the current headlines,** here are a few that have been used in previous debates. Can you feel yourself responding to some of them emotionally? Do they tap into your own personal value system?

Individual vs. Society

- Mandatory drug testing of public officials is justified.

- Community censorship of pornography is justified.

- Contribution to society is the measure of individual worth.

- The public's right to know ought to be valued over national security interests.

Government and Law

- Government by a benevolent dictator is preferable to democracy.

- Laws that protect citizens from themselves are justified.

- Capital punishment is justified.

Foreign Affairs

- The possession of nuclear weapons is immoral.

- The United States ought to value global concerns above its own concerns.

- National interest should be valued over moral principle in the conduct of foreign affairs.

Economics

- Competition is superior to cooperation in achieving excellence.

- Society's obligation to the poor ought to be valued above individual economic freedom.

Environment

- Preserving natural resources for future generations is more important than using them for the present.

- The development of natural resources ought to be valued above the protection of the environment.

Bioethics

- Terminally ill patients have the right to die.

- Suicide ought to be a crime.

- Genetic engineering is immoral.

Education

- A school's right to search students and lockers is more important than a student's right to privacy.

- Public education after high school ought to be a privilege and not a right.

- School censorship of academic material is harmful to the educational development of high school students.

- High school students' right to confidentiality is of greater value than their parents' right to know.

Gender

- The best way to achieve gender equality is to recognize the differences between men and women.

Philosophical Questions

- The sanctity of life ought to be valued over the quality of life.

- Competition is superior to cooperation in achieving excellence.

- You can't always get what you want.

- We treasure what we earn above what we are given.

Let's look at the Lincoln-Douglas topic of "Competition is always better than cooperation in achieving excellence." Look at the difference between these two statements. Which one is more convincing? Why?

ORDINARY	EXTRAORDINARY
While some people believe that competition is the key to getting better at something, I don't agree. Working together is much better.	While some people believe that competition is the key to achieving excellence, I firmly believe that cooperation teaches far better lessons and allows participants to win on several different levels.

Did you notice the difference between these examples? **The extraordinary one isn't just a simple opinion, it is a statement that shows the depth and strength of the opinion.**

Here's another example based on

"Capital punishment is justified."

Look at how just a few simple words change the impact of the statement.

ORDINARY	EXTRAORDINARY
Capital punishment is exactly the kind of sentence a person should get for taking another's life.	Capital punishment may seem to be the appropriate sentence for someone who has taken another person's life. At least until we discover that the judicial system condemned an innocent person.

Which statement got your attention?

Score Card

Score	Rating
47–50	superior
43–46	excellent
39–42	good
35–38	average

From A to 50

If you are doing a Lincoln-Douglas debate in class, your teacher may simply give you a grade ranging from A to F. If the scoring pattern used by judges in official Lincoln-Douglas tournaments is followed, however, the grade might be a little different. Scoring can go as high as 50 points for each one of the speakers. The scoring sheet is divided into four sections: case and analysis; support of issues through evidence and reasoning; delivery and commentary; and the judges' reasons and comments for the decisions they made.

Because the topic for these debates is not known until right before the participants go out to debate, this type is often exciting and fun. To be a part of these debates, you must be able to think fast on your feet and come up with arguments on a topic you may not know a lot about. Judging sometimes comes from the audience itself, with the winner determined by a show of hands.

"In my first debate, I stood up and pointed out that the opposition had made a mistake in saying there were fifty states. Everyone knew there were fifty-one! I noticed that people were laughing at me. Even my partner was smiling, but I didn't know why. I told my parents about it later, and it was no wonder I had made a mistake. My mom thought there were fifty-two, and my dad said forty-nine."

—Nichole Bigley,
former debater

One Format for a Lincoln-Douglas Debate:

So Here's the Scoop

Constructive speech by AFFIRMATIVE team *(state the resolution, define key words/terms, build a case that upholds this value, and present arguments that support your point of view)* — **6 minutes**

Cross-examination by the NEGATIVE team *(answers to all questions go beyond yes or no but are still kept quite brief and specific)* — **3 minutes**

Constructive speech by the NEGATIVE team — **7 minutes**

Cross-examination by the AFFIRMATIVE team — **3 minutes**

First rebuttal by AFFIRMATIVE team *(repeat issues and strengthen, if possible; point out opposition's weaknesses, but no new issues are allowed)* — **4 minutes**

First rebuttal by NEGATIVE team — **6 minutes**

Second rebuttal by AFFIRMATIVE team — **3 minutes**

HELPFUL RESOURCES

For some expert advice and education on Lincoln-Douglas debates, check out the online instructional videos from Debate Central at *http://debate.uvm.edu/learnld.html*. They are free and range in length from thirty-five to fifty-eight minutes.

HIT THE BOOKS

If you'd like to learn more about the original Lincoln-Douglas debates, check out *The Lincoln-Douglas Debates: The First Complete, Unexpurgated Text*, edited by Harold Holzer (Fordham University Press, 2004).

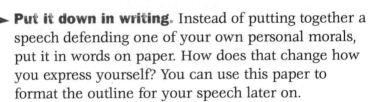

PROJECT JUMP START

★ **Think about your own morals or ethics.** Can you think of a moral statement or an ethic that is important to you? It might be anything from cheating is always wrong or all children need a spanking now and then to everyone has the right to listen to whatever kind of music they want. Write down something that is morally important to you. Now write down five statements that support your opinion. Was it hard to do? Did you find it hard to defend your position?

★ **Put it down in writing.** Instead of putting together a speech defending one of your own personal morals, put it in words on paper. How does that change how you express yourself? You can use this paper to format the outline for your speech later on.

★ **Think fast!** To help you practice thinking fast on your feet, have your friends or family come up with moral issues and respond to each one for sixty seconds without stopping. Watch to see how you improve as you go.

BRAIN JAM:
Lincoln-Douglas Pointers

Look back into history. Check out your library for a video of any televised presidential debates. They are modeled after the Lincoln-Douglas debates. Watch how each candidate handles objections, mistakes, and other challenges.

Pick one, any one. On 3-by-5-inch index cards, write out ten to twenty topics that appeal to you. Put them in a hat or bowl and draw one out. Give yourself five minutes to prepare and then give a three-minute presentation about why you agree or disagree with the statement.

Travel back in time. If you need in-depth information about the history and formatting of Lincoln-Douglas debates, check out *Lincoln-Douglas Debate: Values in Conflict* by Jeffrey Wiese and Stan Lewis (Clark Publishing, 2000). Or visit http://www.perfectionlearning.com/ldd/.

Prime Minister

typical topic

Logic, wit, and
the ability to
persuade

Str

Speaker of the

leader of the oppos.

Logic

Wit

CHAPTER 6

FRANKLIN WATTS

BEING PROPER

Parliamentary Debates

Parliamentary Debates

Although you may think of England when you hear the word *parliamentary*, we have these debates in the United States, too. In this chapter, we will explore:

- **the unique roles in this type of debate;**

- **how parliamentary debates are structured;**

- **typical topics in this kind of debate.**

The United States has its own version of parliamentary debate that originally came from Great Britain's Parliament. In Parliament, spokesmen for the government argue for the affirmative side and the opposition argues for the negative side. This type of debate emphasizes logic, wit, and the ability to persuade others.

What makes this type of debate different?

- Instead of having days, weeks, or months to prepare to debate an issue, the resolution is usually announced about thirty minutes before the debate begins!

- Because there is so little time to prepare, the debate has to be on a topic or idea that most people are familiar with. Traditionally, it is a proverb or quotation centered on general concepts such as love, truth, honor, and courage.

Parliamentary debates are based on the procedures used in the British Parliament. The government team has two players: the prime minister and the member of government. The opposition consists of the leader of the opposition and the member of the opposition. The speaker of the house oversees the entire process. The people debating do not speak directly to each other in this style of debate; they direct their comments to the speaker. For example:

Mr. Speaker, I think that the prime minister's argument is wrong and makes no sense for the following reasons . . .

In this type of debate, you object to or question the opposition's evidence or arguments through the use of a point of information.

"Without the ability to analyze a given situation and discover the particular difficulty to overcome, i.e., the main issue, a man may waste his energy in blind endeavor, like a fly trying to escape through a window."

—William Trufant Foster, author of *The Art of Debating*

In a point of information, a debater on the opponent's team can say, **"Point of information, sir?"** which is a fancy way of saying, **"May I please ask a question?"** They may only ask during constructive speeches, not rebuttals, and they cannot ask during the first or last minute of the speech. The person speaking has the right to say yes or no, but it is considered good manners to say yes at least two times per speech. It is not unusual for someone to ask a question designed to rattle the person speaking.

"I love argument, I love debate. I don't expect anyone just to sit there and agree with me, that's not their job."

—Margaret Thatcher (1925–   )

HIT THE BOOKS

Check out some great sources on parliamentary debate, including *On That Point!: An Introduction to Parliamentary Debate* by John Meany and Kate Shuster (International Debate Education Association, 2003); *Art, Argument, and Advocacy: Mastering Parliamentary Debate* by the same authors (International Debate Education Association, 2002); and *Elements of Parliamentary Debate: A Guide to Public Argument* by Trischa Knapp and Lawrence Galizio (Allyn and Bacon, 1998).

Each round of a parliamentary debate includes a total of six speeches: four constructive speeches and two rebuttals. Here is the typical format:

Prime minister's constructive speech ☞ **7 minutes**

Leader of the opposition's constructive speech ☞ **8 minutes**

Member of government's constructive speech ☞ **8 minutes**

Member of opposition's constructive speech ☞ **8 minutes**

Leader of opposition's rebuttal ☞ **4 minutes**

Prime minister's rebuttal ☞ **5 minutes**

The members of each team have about 20 minutes to make their case and impress the judges. You really need to make those minutes count!

So Here's the Scoop

PROJECT JUMP START

 Proverb time. To practice parliamentary debate, select one of the following proverbs and write out three examples of how you would show it was right or wrong.

- Absence makes the heart grow fonder.

- You are making a mountain out of a molehill.

- Never put all of your eggs in one basket.

May I quote you? Same activity as above, only this time try it with one of these well-known quotations.

- "The unexamined life is not worth living."

- "There never was a good war or a bad peace."

- "No man is an island."

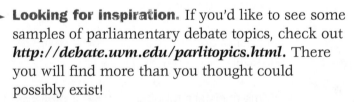 **Looking for inspiration.** If you'd like to see some samples of parliamentary debate topics, check out *http://debate.uvm.edu/parlitopics.html.* There you will find more than you thought could possibly exist!

BRAIN JAM:
Copy the Format

Use the parliamentary format to debate a topic on the Lincoln-Douglas list. How does it change how you respond to others when you have to siphon all of your comments through the speaker of the house?

ime!

Usual format fo

Policy resolut

debate focuses

an issue involv

government pol

Time!

affirmative rebuttal

BEING CURRENT

Policy Resolution Debates

Policy Resolution Debates

The policy resolution debate (also known as the Oregon style, team debate, or team policy debate) requires a lot of time for research and preparation. In this chapter, you will learn how:

- **this type of debate differs from others;**
- **the judges score this type of debate;**
- **the structure of this type of debate is unique.**

The policy resolution style of debate is quite common in college and high school. Students are given a year to prepare for it, and some even go to camp to prepare (see page 121 for a list of debate camps). The debate focuses on an issue involving government policy and not on any basic values or ethics, so it relies very heavily on organization and evidence. There are two people on each team. During the event, the judge takes notes and keeps track of the time, usually signaling the number of minutes left in each round. When the time is up, some will announce, "Time!"

The format of this type of debate is different from all other kinds of debates. Each of the four speakers is awarded as many as five points in each of five different categories.

What's the Score?

Analysis/Organization

Did the speaker identify the main topic? Were the most important issues pointed out? How well was the cross-examination conducted?

Reasoning/Logic/ Evidence

How well did the speaker present his or her side of the issue? Were the opposition's arguments directly addressed? Were the fallacies caught? What was the quality of the cited sources? Was evidence directly applied to the arguments? Was it obvious that the speaker understood the evidence being used?

Delivery

What was the quality of the speaker's clarity, poise, gestures, eye contact, personality, grammar, and overall performance?

Refutation

Did the speaker address all arguments in the debate as well as weaken the opponent's arguments?

Format

Did the student participate in all discussions politely and knowledgeably? Was he or she respectful and cooperative?

There is a possibility of 25 points. Scores of 21–25 are considered very high, while scores of 15–18 are considered quite low. Score sheets usually include commentary and feedback from the judge. Read yours over carefully. It can be very helpful in knowing how to improve your score the next time around.

"My worst moment was my first debate. It truly was a 'baptism by fire.' It was scary because I was a freshman and I was debating a junior. It was completely intimidating. But my best moment was when I realized how much I had grown. I started timid and unsure and ended confident about sharing my ideas."

—Christine Pham, debate coach

The Usual Format for a Policy Resolution Debate

So Here's the Scoop

First affirmative constructive speech	☛ **8 minutes**
Cross-examination	☛ **3 minutes**
First negative constructive speech	☛ **8 minutes**
Cross-examination	☛ **3 minutes**
Second affirmative constructive speech	☛ **8 minutes**
Cross-examination	☛ **3 minutes**
Second negative constructive speech	☛ **8 minutes**
Cross-examination	☛ **3 minutes**
First negative rebuttal	☛ **5 minutes**
First affirmative rebuttal	☛ **5 minutes**
Second negative rebuttal	☛ **5 minutes**
Second affirmative rebuttal	☛ **5 minutes**

PROJECT JUMP START

★ **Politics on the brain.** Think about some of the many current events taking place in the world today. If you were in charge of writing the policy resolution statement for 2006, what would it be? What is your stand on the issue?

★ **Ideas, ideas, ideas.** Go online and check out the Web site *http://www.wfu.edu/organizations/ NDT/HistoricalLists/topics.html*. Here you will see the national policy resolution statements for the last fifty-nine years! Look through the list and pick out the three that sound the most interesting to you.

★ **Topic at hand.** A recent policy resolution was: The United States federal government should establish an energy policy requiring a substantial reduction in the total nongovernmental consumption of fossil fuels in the United States.

Write down at least three points you would have included in your speech for or against this resolution.

BRAIN JAM:
Polish Your Skills

Rent a video. If you want to see a movie and learn about debate at the same time, check out the film *Listen to Me* (1989), starring Kirk Cameron. It focuses on two collegiate debaters.

Off-time practice. Develop a good relationship with your other team members. Stick together. Practice together, even without the coach. This will help you to know each other better and learn how best to support one another in a tournament.

Home page. Make your home page on your computer one of the major news sites so that you can see the front-page headlines every day. It will help you keep up on political events that may have an effect on the issue you are debating.

Humorous

Dramatic

Heckling debate,

tournament

Dema

Stress

Duo interpr

Original ora

expository

Victories

FRANKLIN

CHAPTER 8

WATTS

BEING ON TARGET

Other Types of Debates and Speech Competitions

Other Types of Debates and Speech Competitions

There are many other types of competitions that take place at debate and speech tournaments. This chapter will tell you about:

- **heckling debates;**

- **original oratory;**

- **humorous, dramatic, and duo interpretations;**

- **expository;**

- **what it is like to be in a debate tournament.**

The world of forensics is both large and always changing. According to Joe Patrice, a former debater and now a lawyer in New York, the collegiate world is really expanding the definition of debate. "At California State University in Long Beach, some teams are debating in the hip-hop and rap style almost exclusively," he says. "The University of Louisville has an African-American team that is debating in the style of gospel ministers." It is likely that these new styles—and others—will eventually filter down to the high school level.

Competition Categories

Speaking in public can take many directions other than debate. Here is a look at a few of the main ones. Do any of them leap off the page and shout, "Hey! This is the one for me!"?

The heckling debate is similar to what is done in a legislative debate in the House of Representatives and Senate. (If you do not like being interrupted when you are talking, this style may drive you nuts!) Speakers from each side of an issue can be interrupted by members of the opposing team, stating aloud, **"Will the speaker yield for a question?"** The question is superfluous; according to the rules, the speaker must always say yes.

During the constructive speech, a heckler can interrupt as many as four times after the third minute and before the eighth minute. These periods are pointed out by the timekeeper, whose job it is to announce **"Heckling may begin" or "Heckling must cease."** The heckler may even interrupt two times during the rebuttal. There are some limits on the heckler, however. Questions must be brief and to the point.

Original oratory is another kind of public speaking that is often part of a forensics tournament. In this event, you write a speech that can persuade, inform, or just entertain. You memorize it and then deliver it in front of a judge. Most events are eight to ten minutes long, and students commonly pick a topic that they are quite passionate about. This is the only formal debating format in which you get to choose the topic.

Here are two examples of oratory speech. Look at the difference between them. Which one would be more likely to move you to tears?

ORDINARY	EXTRAORDINARY
I am tired of fighting. My people are all defeated. They are cold and hungry. Some have run away. I need to find and take care of all of them. I will fight no more.	"I am tired of fighting. Our Chiefs are killed. . . . The old men are all dead. It is the young men who say yes or no. He who led the young men is dead. It is cold, and we have no blankets; the little children are freezing to death. My people. Some of them, have run away to the hills, and have no blankets, no food. No one knows where they are—perhaps freezing to death. I want to have time to look for my children, and see how many of them I can find. Maybe I shall find them among the dead. Hear me, my Chiefs! I am tired; my heart is sick and sad. From where the sun now stands I will fight no more forever." —*Chief Joseph*

More Competition Categories

Humorous interpretation competition consists of a ten-minute performance in which you are acting out an amusing excerpt from a stage play, film, or radio broadcast. A dramatic interpretation is the same thing, only it is dramatic rather than funny. If you perform this with a partner, it is called (not too surprisingly) a duo interpretation.

Expository is a form of speaking that calls for thinking fast on your feet. You are given three topics in current events to choose from. Once you have made your choice, you have approximately thirty minutes to put together a speech about it.

And Now a Word about Tournaments

If you enjoy debate enough—or if you just feel up to a challenge—you might end up going to a debate tournament at the local, state, or even national level. These tournaments are offered at different levels, from novice to experienced. Are you ready to imagine being on the debate version of *American Idol*?

Debate tournaments are like any other competitive event: full of stress, demands, victories, and losses. They are commonly held out of town, and you and your team must travel to the site of the event. Because these events are often held on weekends, you need to ask yourself if you are willing to give up your free days before signing up for these competitions. If you decide to participate, you will have an amazing opportunity to:

- **set personal goals,**
- **show off your skills,**
- **shine!**

Taking Care of Yourself

Tournaments can run from one to seven days and can be physically and mentally exhausting. You need to take care of yourself and that means:

Sleeping as much as possible. These trips are a chance to compete, not party. Shall we all repeat that? It is NOT a party.

Preparing thoroughly before you go so you are not studying while in transit or between rounds.

Bringing something to do that is not debate related for your downtime between rounds. Reading a book or magazine, listening to a portable audio player, or playing a handheld video game will give you something else to focus on and help you to relax.

Watching people in other rounds and seeing what you can learn from them.

Eating healthy food and drinking plenty of water so that your voice stays strong.

Considering using a humidifier in your room to protect your voice or drinking an occasional cup of hot tea with honey.

Preparing physically for the stress of the tournament by using positive visualizations, stretching, singing to loosen your voice, and taking deep breaths.

The judges at tournaments are usually a mixture of debate coaches, former competitors, and adult volunteers. They fill out ballots or evaluation forms on all of the participants. Prepare for them to be somewhat consistently inconsistent, but also remember that it is never the judges' fault if you get a poor ranking. "Perhaps my hardest moments in debate are as a judge," says Miranda Weigler, a debate coach at Colgate University in New York. "It is so hard to tell someone he or she did not win a round. It's difficult dealing with that niggle of doubt in your mind."

"There are a few things you can do to help you succeed in formal competition and take home more than your fair share of awards, no matter which event you choose.
1) Work hard
2) Work hard
3) Work hard"

—Brent C. Oberg, author of *Forensics: The Winner's Guide to Speech Contests*

How Do I Look?

Your appearance and behavior at a tournament are important. **Be sure to dress professionally** (this is not the time to try out the new purple boa or the jeans that fall down if you walk too quickly) **and act professionally.** Even though it might be fun to fool around with friends before, between, and after rounds, you never know if the person sharing your hotel elevator or sitting in the restaurant may be one of your judges.

How Do I Feel?

If you are not nervous before a tournament, something is wrong. Remember that **anxiety can enhance your performance if you let it.** It will give you the adrenaline edge you need to be at your best. There is a great positive affirmation that says, "To become, act as if." If you want to become calm, confident, and competent, imagine that you already are. Pretending can often lead you right to reality.

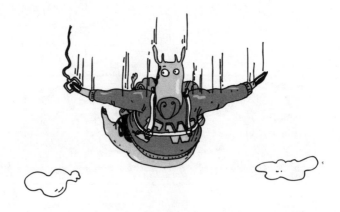

Tournament Tales

Chris Richter, half of the team that won the 2002
National Champions of NPDA in Colorado and current
debate coach at Portland State University in Oregon,
recalls his first tournament. "I wanted to learn how
to argue because I felt I had a natural aptitude for it,"
he says with a chuckle. "I was thrown into my first
tournament as a 'wild card.' I had no idea what I was
doing, and I lost every round. But now I knew how the
game was played." He and his partner, Ben Garcia, went
on to win many different levels of debate and were
offered debate scholarships to the University of Alaska
in Anchorage.

TIP FILE

The difference between a mediocre debater
and an extraordinary debater is how that
person reacts to the judge and audience.
Debaters must learn to read judges and react
accordingly by making jokes, elaborating on
a point the judge seems extra interested in,
or moving on when the judge has clearly
gotten the point.

"It is hard to believe that on a campus where you can be killed by a moose that debate is big, but it is," says Garcia. Today, Garcia is assistant debate coach at Portland State University and is also majoring in law at Lewis and Clark University. **"I received a full tuition waiver for school, and I squarely blame debate for that,"** he says with a grin.

Dr. Mabry O'Donnell is a forensics instructor at Marietta College in Ohio. She has been in the field for more than thirty years. **"Tournaments will teach students more about debate than any other lesson,"** she says. "I did learn you have to remind them of many things, however. We were on the way to a tournament in Virginia, and my team was made up of all young men. They were quite proud that they had all brought their research, notes, and other details. However, not one remembered clean underwear."

TIP FILE

How do you deal with losing? Remember that even the best debaters often had abysmal records when they started out. It is normal. There is light at the end of the tunnel, though. Always keep in mind that losing is not a reflection of your life or yourself. Glory in the art and experience of the competition instead of just focusing on winning.

HIT THE BOOKS

For more information on debating in front of an audience, head to the library and check out *Argument and Audience: Presenting Debates in Public Settings* by Ken Broda-Bahm, Daniela Kempf, and William J. Driscoll (International Debate Education Association, 2004).

"Freedom is hammered out on the anvil of discussion, dissent, and debate."

—Hubert H. Humphrey (1911–1978)

PROJECT JUMP START

★ **Keepin' it straight in the world of debate.** Imagine taking a debate topic and putting it into a completely different style. How might you write it in rap? How would an evangelist perform it? A rock star? If you could choose any style, what would it be?

 Pick an interpretation. Select a scene you would like to perform. Would it be a humorous one? Dramatic? Would you like to do it with a partner for a duo interpretation?

 Quick on your feet. Imagine that you have been given these four topics to talk about. Which one would you pick? What are the first three points you would make about it?

- The driving age should be raised to eighteen.

- All colleges should be free.

- Animals should never be killed for food.

- Computers have forced people further apart.

BRAIN JAM:
Tournament Prep

Digging deeper. To find out about the different kinds of competitive speech available, check out the book *Forensics: The Winner's Guide to Speech Contests* by Brent C. Oberg (Meriwether Publishing, 1995).

Ask around. Check with your school and other schools in your city to see if any of them will be holding a local debate tournament. If there is one, be sure to take the time to go to it. Watch what happens and see if it is something you would like to try.

Write it out. Imagine that you are going to do an oratory speech. Select a topic and write the first paragraph of it. Read it and then go back and change the verbs to more powerful ones. Add adjectives. Put in passion, conviction, and emotion. Read it again. How is it different?

TO FIND OUT MORE

Books

Branham, Robert. *Debate and Critical Analysis: The Harmony of Conflict.* Hillsdale, NJ: Erlbaum, 1991.

Dunbar, Robert E. *How to Debate.* New York: Franklin Watts, 1994.

Freely, Austin. *Argumentation and Debate: Critical Thinking for Reasoned Decision Making.* Belmont, NY: Wadsworth, 2004.

Kushner, Malcolm. *Public Speaking for Dummies.* Indianapolis: Wiley Publishing Co., 2004.

Oberg, Brent C. *Forensics: The Winner's Guide to Speech Contests.* Colorado Springs, CO: Meriwether Publishing Ltd., 1995.

Sather, Trevor, ed. *Pros and Cons: A Debater's Handbook.* New York: Routledge, 1999.

Debate Camps

Debate Camp Canada
Shawnigan Lake, British Columbia
888-512-8154

Jefferson Public Speaking Institute
Berkeley, California
510-548-6612

Leadership in Character Summer Institute
Rockville, Maryland
410-756-1456

National Debate Institute
New York, New York
510-548-4800

Speech and Debate Institute
Dayton, Ohio
513-873-3135

World Debate Institute
Burlington, Vermont
802-656-4275

Tournament Information

Annual Debate Tournament of the Catholic Forensic League

Secretary-Treasurer
Catholic Forensic League
Natick High School
Natick, MA 01760

Harvard Debate Tournament

Quincy House
Harvard University
Cambridge MA 02138

National Speech and Debate Tournament

National Forensic League
PO Box 38
Ripon, WI 54971

Tournament of Champions

Director of Debate
University of Kentucky
Lexington, KY 40506

Organizations and Online Sites

American Forensic Association
http://www.americanforensics.org/

Visit the site of the American Forensic Association, whose mission in part is "to expand students' appreciation for the place of argument and advocacy in shaping their worlds, and to prepare students through classrooms, forums, and competition for participation in their world through the power of expression."

Cross Examination Debate Association
http://cedadebate.org/home.htm

A college debate organization whose goal is to "serve as a professional association for scholars and teachers in the field of applied argumentation and debate."

Debate Central
http://debate.uvm.edu

A resource for students and teachers with information on coaching, speaking, and research as well as online debate videos.

National Association of Urban Debate Leagues
http://urbandebate.org/

The goal of the National Association of Urban Debate Leagues is to "improve urban public education by empowering youth to become engaged learners, critical thinkers, and active citizens who are effective advocates for themselves and their communities."

National Debate Coaches Association
http://www.thendca.com

Although it is primarily geared to help debate coaches, it has some excellent information.

National Debate Tournament
http://www.wfu.edu/organizations/NDT/
Visit this site to learn more about the National Debate
Tournament.

National Forensic League
http://www.nflonline.org/AboutNFL/Contact
Visit this site for information about the National
Forensic League and its mission.

Planet Debate
http://www.planetdebate.com/
A source for downloading and purchasing guides, documents, and other educational material for those interested in debate. The site was started by a group of Harvard
debate graduates.

INDEX

TAMRA B. ORR

ABOUT THE AUTHOR

I live in Portland, Oregon. I have written more than fifty nonfiction books as well as lots and lots of magazine articles, educational tests, and even some board game cards!

Debating would have terrified me in school. I was the kind of student who struggled to get up the nerve to order a pizza over the phone. Standing up in front of the classroom and speaking was terror-inducing. Unlike many of you reading this book, I never had a teacher say, "Hey, you know debate could help you deal with some of these public speaking anxiety issues." I wish they had.

My initiation into public speaking came in a truly ironic way. I was hired by a local community college to teach a course on composition. While I was preparing to teach this course, the teacher slated to teach public speech quit. The college called me to see if I could start teaching the course in two weeks. Being the fool that I was, however, I said, "Sure!" When I finally stopped beating my head against the wall, I made a plan. I joined Toastmaster's, an international organization dedicated to helping people become strong public speakers. I took a crash course and learned the basics. Two weeks later, I strolled into class and did my best to never let them see me sweat. Since then, I have gone on to appear on radio and television and in front of an audience of several hundred people. (My parents are still in shock.)

Debate teaches you the confidence, competence, and curiosity for knowledge that you will access over and over. Whatever field you go into, you will find times when you will need to present facts in an organized manner and stand up to opposing forces. Debate shows you how to do that—and do it well. In my case, I use debating skills now and then with editors, here and there with publishers, and hourly with my four children. Wishing you wise words!